THE BOYNE OBELISK

From a photograph

IRISH

STREET SONGS AND BALLADS

By
John Hand

Fredonia Books
Amsterdam, The Netherlands

Irish Street Songs and Ballads

by
John Hand

ISBN: 1-4101-0740-X

Copyright © 2004 by Fredonia Books

Fredonia Books
Amsterdam, The Netherlands
http://www.fredoniabooks.com

In order to make original editions of historical works
available to scholars at an economical price, this
facsimile of the original edition is reproduced from
the best available copy and has been digitally
enhanced to improve legibility, but the text remains
unaltered to retain historical authenticity.

IRISH

STREET SONGS AND BALLADS

STREET SONGS AND BALLADS AND ANONYMOUS VERSE.

BY JOHN HAND.

IRELAND owes much to her ballad poetry, and not a little to tha portion of it which is associated with the streets. Most, if not all, nations owe more or less to poetry. The songs of Homer, even more than her banded might, preserved Greece independent for over a thousand years. The ballads of Spain kept Spanish patriotism brightly burning thoughout the centuries which saw the Moor rooted in the land, and finally, by the potency of their magic, swept Boabdil and his legions from Granada—from Spain—tore down the Crescent from the high places of the Saracen, and raised in its stead once again the glorious emblem of man's salvation—the Cross of the Redeemer. For Ireland, the ballad and the song have done more than for even Spain or Greece. It is true, she has not obtained a result so significantly brilliant as that achieved by Spain. She has not succeeded, after all her struggles, in shaking herself free of the foreigner's yoke. Spain, like Ireland, was seized and held by a foreign foe ; but that foe, though infidel, was less rapacious and less brutal than the pretentious Christian one that fastened upon Ireland. The Moor was the patron of learning, and gave almost lavish encouragement to the arts and sciences in the celebrated schools which he established at Cordova and throughout Spain.

The Englishman's instruments of civilization in Ireland were the sword and the halter—the destruction of her schools, the violation and robbery of her sanctuaries, the outlawry of her language and its teachers. It was not the province of England to build up, to foster and encourage learning there, but to despoil, to destroy, and to brutalize, by every means that the dark fiend himself might suggest, the Irish race, because, forsooth, the children of that race refused to reach out their arms, and meekly receive the shackles of the slave. Learning was banned in Ireland, but the Irish mother, with a fervor almost amounting to religious devotion, taught her child the old ballads and songs which told of Ireland and of Ireland's faith, and which her own mother in a similar way had taught to her. From Cape Clear to the Giant's Causeway, in every peasant homestead throughout the length and the breadth of the land, were those songs sung and those ballads conned over. Under God they have been the means of preserving her nationality and her faith through centuries of disasters and persecutions such as a nation never before suffered and survived. When English laws put the ban of outlawry on her bards, and finally destroyed them, did England even then succeed in her nefarious design ? No !—the song lived, though the lips that first chanted it were silent for ever. The ballad never lost its significance or its power ; generation after generation were swayed by the magic of its numbers—the fierceness of its invective, the pathos of its love, or the wild agony of its wail, still exercised the same talismanic effect on the Irish heart.

1

The Irish language, with its graceful idioms and epigrammatic terseness, was peculiarly adapted for poetry. Even when fairly translated into the English tongue, much of the beauty of the original is perceptible. What a magnificent ballad have we not in poor Clarence Mangan's beautiful translation of ' Dark Rosaleen.' It is unsurpassed by any ballad of any language—a real gem—classic as Homer. . . .

It was to such ballads as this Ireland was accustomed prior to that long night of darkness and agony which set in upon her with the reign of England's Elizabeth. Such were her "Streets Ballads" in those days ; and it can be readily imagined what an effect such a ballad as ' Dark Rosaleen,' sung or recited in the native tongue, would have on the excitable Irish temperament—how it would stir, how it would fascinate, how it would impress and mold, the susceptible Irish heart. Why, even in the foreign tongue, in the heavy, and by no means poetical language of England, the blood runs faster as it is declaimed—it carries you along in its grand flow, and its every impassioned sentiment becomes your own. But in the old tongue in the language of the land, the effect of a such a ballad would be magical.

Since the days when it became treason to love their country, the Irish bards usually adopted allegory, such as we find in ' Dark Rosaleen.' They sang of Ireland as the ' Dark Little Rose,' the ' Shan Van Vocht,' the ' Coolin,' and under a hundred other names. A great writer has said that the Irish are one of the most poetic of the peoples on earth ; that in them is the true spirit poetry to be found. With an old, brave race, such as the Irish, having grand traditions and proud memories, it could scarcely be other. Nature is the great rudimentary school in which poetry is imbibed; and in " green Erin of the streams " the child of the land is ever present face to face with the high teacher, in what mood soever she chooses to array herself. And though he may never measure a line of poetry, or indeed know the difference between *iambics* and the Hill of Howth, he is not the less a poet, for his soul drinks in the glories of nature, and responds to her thousand fitful but always beautiful aspects.

Ireland has been happily termed the " land of song." In the pre-Christian, as in the Christian era, song was her delight, and she delighted to excel in the art. It swayed her with a certainty as true as the moon sways the tides. . . .

Nine out of every ten men you meet with in Ireland are poets ; and the tenth man will, in all probability, be a Saxon or other " benighted foreigner." The majority of them, however, it need scarcely be added, remain " mute inglorious Miltons," but might, and no doubt would, under different circumstances become glorious ones. In Ireland, rustic bards swarm thick as blackberries in harvest-time, and not a few of the craft have we ourselves personally known. As in every other department, so in the rhyming trade, there is always to be found in each parish or district a workman superior to his fellows. . . .

The Irish street ballad proper was on every conceivable subject—embraced love, politics, religion, war, shipwreck, in fact, took in the whole range of creation—sun, moon, stars, skies, and the earth, with all its belongings, but more particularly that delightful portion of it ycleped the "Emerald Isle." Indeed it was no uncommon thing for a countryman, on being asked to sing, to inquire on what subject the company would wish him to oblige—whether they would have a love, or love-and-murder, a "rale ould Irish" (meaning a national), a controversial, or a sea song. We have often heard the question asked in this way, when the minstrel would take his cue from the majority, and treat them to what they liked best.

Love was a deity the rustic bard very frequently bowed before. Her he invoked, and to her he poured out the woes of his wounded spirit in swelling numbers. Here is one who tells us he came a stranger to the country about Ardee, where he lost his heart. He thus makes us acquainted with the sad tale :

> "When first to this country a stranger I came,
> I placed my affections on a comely fair maid,
> She was proper, tall and handsome, in every degree,
> She's the flower of this country, and the Rose of Ardee.

> "I courted lovely Mary at the age of sixteen,
> Her waist it was slender, and her carriage genteel ;
> Till at length a young weaver came for her to see,
> Stole the flower of this country and the Rose of Ardee."

Poor fellow, this was a sad ending to his dreams. Though the provocation was great, he did not commit suicide, however. After cursing the weaver "by day and by night," he proceeds—

> "When I get my week's wages to the *Shebeen* I'll go,
> And there I'll sit drinkin' with my heart full of woe,
> I'll sit there lamentin', expectin' to see
> Once more my own true love, the Rose of Ardee."

After a good deal of "lamenting," the bard arrives at a philosophic conclusion, and ends by bidding his false fair one an eternal farewell.

> "Farewell, lovely Mary, tho' fled from my sight,
> For you I am weepin' by day and by night,
> For I fear my sweet angel I never shall see,
> So adieu evermore to the Rose of Ardee."

There is another characteristic effusion, entitled the 'Star of Slane.' Observe how the bard displays his knowledge of history and mythology. It is so loaded with classic allusions that, like the "other" straw breaking the camel's back, one other would be more than it could actually bear. Bright Sol, Paris, the Grecian Queen, Troy, Cæsar, Cleopatra, Alexander, Cupid, Diana, Susanna, and the River Boyne, are all marshaled up to give effect.

This was the style of versification most admired, particularly when the words were, as here, of "learned length and thundering sound."

Who but an Irish street-balladist could express affection for the angel of his love in so happy a manner as does the wooer of Peggy Brady ? What colleen but would melt at so moving and so artless an assurance. The unselfishness of the declaration is most refreshing read in an age sordid as the present.

> "O Peggy Brady, you are my darlin',
> You are my lookin'-glass from night to mornin',
> I 'd rather have you without a farthin'
> Than Susy Gallagher, wid her house and garden."

The polemical ballad was always in high favor. The Church was persecuted with fiendish malignity ; and the people loved and clung to her the more for that very persecution. Innumerable were the ballads written in her behalf, or portraying her sufferings—the majority of them, from a literary point of view, being the very quintessence of absurdity ; yet they were disseminated and sung, and kept the subject ever green in the susceptible hearts of the Irish peasantry. Of the religious class, the controversial was perhaps most admired. It gave scope to the bard for the display of his biblical lore and sublime invective, qualities altogether indispensable to the rustic muse. " One morning in July," the poet tells us —he was " ranging" over " Urker Hill," when a church and chapel adjacent had a regular "set to"—to use a modern phrase. The Protestant church was the aggressor on the occasion, scornfully alluding to the poverty-stricken appearance of her rival. But she had evidently calculated without her host, for the chapel, putting forth all her powers, administered her such a drubbing as Lutheran structure never received before. The church had made some grave charges, but,

> "The prudent chapel then made answer,
> And was not angry, nor yet confused,
> Sayin', madam, sittin' in yer pomp an' grandeur,
> I beg the favor to be excused,
> I do renegade and flatter none,
> I was erected by true Milesians,
> An' my ordination is the Church of Rome ! "

This was an effective hit, but is even surpassed by what follows.

> "I do remimber, in former ages,
> Whin you wur naked as well as I,
> Till by false teachin' ye did invade us
> By prachin' doctrines of heresy."

Needless to say that under such admirably administered castigation, the church was forced to succumb.

'The Ass and the Orangeman's Daughter,' as the title implies, was another classic production. It proved, besides, a mine of wealth —a very Golconda—to scores of street minstrels.

Few public men had more ballads written about them than Daniel O'Connell. For fully forty years every town and hamlet in Ireland was flooded with poetic effusions in praise of the Liberator.

The death of O'Connell, all unexpected as it was, produced a deep sensation throughout Ireland, and plunged the entire country into profound grief.

The national grief found expression in divers ways, and not the least sincere and real was its burden as uttered through the verse of the rustic bard, and sang through the streets of every town and village in the land. Some of these ballads had a prodigious sale—not less than a million copies of several of them being sold in an incredibly short space of time. 'Erin's Lament' ran through countless editions. Large crowds used to surround the street minstrel as, with stentorian lungs, he poured forth the words of the ballad, which, by the way, were attached to a beautiful and plaintive melody. The ballads were purchased as fast as they could be handed out. The singer generally sang the song right through, and then started afresh as follows :—

> " One morning ranging for recreation,
>   Down by a river I chanced to rove,
> Where I espied a maiden in conversation,
>   Just quite adjacent to a shady grove ;
> I was struck with wonder, so I stood and pondered,
>   I could stand no longer, so I just stept o'er,
> And the song she sung made the valleys ring,
>   It was Erin's King, brave Dan 's no more.

> " When I heard the news I was much confused ;
>   And myself excused, when this I did say,
> Is O'Connell gone, old Granua's son ?
>   The brightest orb that e'er stood the day ;
> To relate his glory, his name 's famed in story,
>   Whilst Erin will sorely feel the fall,
> For his sweet voice will no more rejoice,
>   Whilst our harp quite mute lies in Tara's hall."

In a similar fashion are reviewed the principal incidents in the career of the departed ; and the song relates that

> " The Emancipation, without hesitation,
>   To our lovely island he soon brought o'er,
> And our clergy crowned him with wreaths of glory,
>   When that he sailed to Old Erin's shore ;
> Our chapel bells they do ring melodious,
>   Where no vile scorpion dare cross the door ;
> Quite broken hearted, from us departed,
>   The pride of Kerry, brave Dan 's no more."

The 'Rights of Man' is another allegorical effusion. The bard had a vision, and among other phenomena the following quaint picture is limned :

> " Through the azure sky I then did spy
>   A man to fly and for to descend,
> And lights came down upon the ground
>   Where Erin round had her bosom friends ;
> His dazzling miter and cross was brighter
>   Than stars by night or the mid-day sun,
> In accents rare then I do declare
>   He prayed sincere for the rights of man."

Again we have 'The Banished Defender,' in which politics, religion, and pikes are beautifully mingled. In the first verse the poet tells us he is fled to the mountains, and in the next—probably forgetting what he had told us in the former—we are assured that he is a convict in Van Dieman's Land. Here is a sample:—

" You Catholics of Erin, give ear unto these lines I write,
I 've fled unto the mountains, for ever I am banished quite ;
For the sake of my religion, I 'm bound to leave my native home,
For being a bold defender, and a member of the Church of Rome.

Then woe attend those traitors that forced me from my native shore,
Those perjured prosecutors that has me banished for evermore.
They say I was a traitor, and a leader of the Papist band,
For which I'm in cold irons, a convict in Van Dieman's land."

He knows something of theology, as the following extract will show:

" Transubstantiation is the faith we depend upon,
Look and you will find it in the fifth chapter of St. John,
As Moses and Elias they told us of our heavenly church,
That we in future ages should suffer persecution much."

The gentleman who penned the following must have risen fresh from the study of Virgil, his mind all aglow with the stately harmony he found in the Latin poet. How else could he sing—

" Near Castleblayney, lived Dan Delaney,
And the broth of a boy was Pat McCann"?

Observe the harmonious connection. We have it that " Dan Delaney " lived near Castleblayney, and in the same breath are assured of the important fact that

"The broth of a boy was Pat McCann."

Who could doubt it ? or doubt the versatile genius and originality of the poet who, with this single touch, dubs the above worthies immortal?

'McKenna's Dream,' 'Brannon on the Moor,' 'Bold Traynor O,' 'Donnelly and Cooper,' 'The River Roe,' 'My Brown Girl Sweet,' and 'Lovely Mary of the Shannon Side,' have had an immense run in their day, and have been sung from the Hill of Howth to the wild shores of Arran, and from Slieve-na-mon to the weird peaked mountain of Donegal.

This class of ballads is now rapidly fading away—becoming fast obsolete before the spread of a better education. The ballad to be sold now in Ireland must have literary merit, and instead of the 'Bold Defender,' the 'Rights of Man,' the 'Star of Slane,' etc., inquiries are made for ' O'Donnell Abu,' ' Rory of the Hills,' ' God Save Ireland,' 'Gra-gal-Machree,' 'Brian the Brave,' 'Rich and Rare,' and other of the sparkling gems of Thomas Moore. The old street-ballads are dying—smooth be their passage to oblivion. They had their day, and performed their mission well. They lived in a rugged time; and recalled many a wavering heart, in their own rude fashion, to a sense of duty. They can now only survive in the sketch book of a Carleton, or other delineator of the Irish of a past generation. Yet among the street ballads proper are to be found stray pearlets that must and will survive. Many such there are that cannot and should not be allowed to depart from amongst us !

Happily there are ballads to take the place of the dead or dying ones. Instead of the ' Rose of Ardee,' and others of that ilk, we have

'Cushla Gal Machree,' from the pen of brave-hearted Michael Doheny, the ballads of hopeful, earnest-souled Thomas Davis,—ballads that thrill you like an inspiration—the weird but melodious productions of the muse of Clarence Mangan, and all the varied and magnificent treasure of 'Young Ireland.' 'Forty-eight saw the commencement of a new era in Irish ballad poetry.

The tocsin was sounded by Mangan in 'The Nation's First Number.' A wave of the magic wand of Thomas Davis, and the accumulated poetical absurdities, in the shape of the accepted street ballad, were swept away in the flood which his great and impassioned genius had conjured. The rustic song maker found his occupation gone ; for who of the new generation—all of whom had or were receiving more or less of an education—would buy or read such an effusion, for instance, as ' Mary Neal ' ?

'Mary Neal' went " out of print." The freshened ideas of " Young Ireland " extinguished it and all of its class. Who would buy such when a song like this could be purchased ?

" Come in the evening, or come in the morning,
    Come when you 're looked for, or come without warning ;
    Kisses and welcome you 'll have here before ye,
    And the oftener you come here the more I 'll adore ye."

'The Blackbird,' the 'Shan Van Vocht,' and such other of the *genus* political, were literally snuffed out by the grand march forward then inaugurated. The hopeful, melodious, glowing, and martial verse of Gavan Duffy, D'Arcy Magee, Dalton Williams, Lady Wilde, and all that brilliant phalanx who gave to the period such a luster, contributed to this desired event.

The old street ballads are gone ; with many of them were associated pleasant memories. May the pleasure remain, but what of them was rancorous, uncharitable, bigoted, or envenomed, pass away, and be buried in the same oblivious grave.

" Give me the making of a people's ballads, and I care not who make their laws," was the saying of an ancient philosopher, and the wisdom of old Fletcher of Saltoun, author of the saying, was never better exemplified than in the case of Ireland. Her nationality has been preserved by the aid of her ballads ; seeing what they have accomplished, may we not safely predict that the potency of their magic will yet help to consummate what for centuries has been her fixed and grand idea—Ireland a Nation—the arbiter of her own destinies ?

THE BOYNE WATER.[1]

July the First, of a morning clear one thousand six hundred
        and ninety,
King William did his men prepare—of thousands he had
        thirty—

[1] Sir Charles Gavan Duffy says these fragments of the original ' Boyne Water ' are far more racy and spirited than the song by Colonel Blacker which has superseded them.

To fight King James and all his foes, encamped near the Boyne
Water

He little feared, though two to one, their multitudes to scatter.

King William called his officers, saying: " Gentlemen, mind
your station,

And let your valor here be shown before this Irish nation;

My brazen walls let no man break, and your subtle foes you 'll
scatter,

Be sure you show them good English play as you go over the
water."

. . . . . .

Both foot and horse they marched on, intending them to batter,

But the brave Duke Schomberg he was shot as he crossed over
the water.

When that King William did observe the brave Duke Schomberg falling,

He reined his horse with a heavy heart, on the Enniskilleners
calling:

" What will you do for me, brave boys—see yonder men retreat-
ing?

Our enemies encouraged are, and English drums are beating."

He says, " My boys, feel no dismay at the losing of one commander,

For God shall be our king this day, and I 'll be general under."

. . . . . .

Within four yards of our fore-front, before a shot was fired,

A sudden snuff they got that day, which little they desired;

For horse and man fell to the ground, and some hung in their
saddle:

Others turned up their forked ends, which we call *coup de
ladle.*

Prince Eugene's regiment was the next, on our right hand ad-
vanced,

Into a field of standing wheat, where Irish horses pranced—

But the brandy ran so in their heads, their senses all did
scatter,

They little thought to leave their bones that day at the Boyne
Water.

Both men and horse lay on the ground, and many there lay
bleeding,

I saw no sickles there that day—but, sure, there was sharp
shearing.

Now, praise God, all true Protestants, and heaven's and earth's
    Creator,
For the deliverance that He sent our enemies to scatter. . . .
The Church's foes will pine away, like churlish-hearted Nabal
For our deliverer came this day like the great Zorobabel.

So praise God, all true Protestants, and I will say no further,
But had the Papists gained the day, there would have been open
    murder.
Although King James and many more were ne'er that way in-
    clined,
It was not in their power to stop what the rabble they designed.

BRIAN O'LINN.[1]

Brian O'Linn was a gentleman born,
His hair it was long and his beard unshorn,
His teeth were out and his eyes far in—
"I'm a wonderful beauty," says Brian O'Linn!

Brian O'Linn was hard up for a coat,
He borrowed the skin of a neighboring goat,
He buckled the horns right under his chin—
"They'll answer for pistols," says Brian O'Linn!

Brian O'Linn had no breeches to wear,
He got him a sheepskin to make him a pair,
With the fleshy side out and the woolly side in—
"They are pleasant and cool," says Brian O'Linn!

Brian O'Linn had no hat to his head,
He stuck on a pot that was under the shed,
He murdered a cod for the sake of his fin—
"'T will pass for a feather," says Brian O'Linn!

Brian O'Linn had no shirt to his back,
He went to a neighbor and borrowed a sack,
He puckered a meal-bag under his chin—
"They'll take it for ruffles," says Brian O'Linn!

Brian O'Linn had no shoes at all,
He bought an old pair at a cobbler's stall,

[1] This version is made up from several in the possession of Mr. P. J.
McCall, of Dublin. The last verse figures in most collections of 'The
Rhymes and Jingles of Mother Goose.'

The uppers were broke and the soles were thin—
"They 'll do me for dancing," says Brian O'Linn!

Brian O'Linn had no watch for to wear,
He bought a fine turnip and scooped it out fair,
He slipped a live cricket right under the skin—
"They 'll think it is ticking," says Brian O'Linn!

Brian O'Linn was in want of a brooch,
He stuck a brass pin in a big cockroach,
The breast of his shirt he fixed it straight in—
"They 'll think it 's a diamond," says Brian O'Linn!

Brian O'Linn went a-courting one night,
He set both the mother and daughter to fight—
"Stop, stop," he exclaimed, "if you have but the tin,
I 'll marry you both," says Brian O'Linn!

Brian O'Linn went to bring his wife home,
He had but one horse, that was all skin and bone—
"I 'll put her behind me, as nate as a pin,
And her mother before me," says Brian O'Linn!

Brian O'Linn and his wife and wife's mother,
They all crossed over the bridge together,
The bridge broke down and they all tumbled in—
"We 'll go home by water," says Brian O'Linn!

BY MEMORY INSPIRED.

By memory inspired
And love of country fired,
The deeds of MEN I love to dwell upon;
And the patriotic glow
Of my Spirit must bestow
A tribute to O'Connell that is gone, boys—gone.
Here 's a memory to the friends that are gone!

In October 'Ninety-Seven—
May his soul find rest in Heaven!—
William Orr to execution was led on:
The jury, drunk, agreed
That IRISH was his creed:
For perjury and threats drove them on, boys—on.
Here 's the memory of John Mitchel that is gone!

In 'Ninety-Eight—the month July—
The informer's pay was high;
When Reynolds gave the gallows brave MacCann;
But MacCann was Reynolds' first—
One could not allay his thirst;
So he brought up Bond and Byrne that are gone, boys—gone.
Here 's the memory of the friends that are gone!

We saw a nation's tears
Shed for John and Henry Sheares;
Betrayed by Judas, Captain Armstrong:
We may forgive, but yet
We never can forget
The poisoning of Maguire [1] that is gone, boys—gone:
Our high Star and true Apostle that is gone!

How did Lord Edward die?
Like a man, without a sigh!
But he left his handiwork on Major Swan!
But Sirr, with steel-clad breast
And coward heart at best,
Left us cause to mourn Lord Edward that is gone, boys—gone.
Here 's the memory of our friends that are gone!

September, Eighteen-Three,
Closed this cruel history,
When Emmet's blood the scaffold flowed upon.
Oh, had their spirits been wise,
They might then realize
Their freedom—but we drink to Emmet that is gone, boys—
gone.
Here 's the memory of the friends that are gone!

————

CHARMING MARY NEAL.

I 'm a bold undaunted Irishman, my name is John McCann.
I 'm a native of sweet Donegal, convenient to Strabane;
For the stealing of an heiress, I lie in Lifford Jail
And her father swears he will me hang for his daughter Mary
Neal.

Whilst in cold irons I lay bound, my love sent word to me:
"Don't fear my father's anger, for I will set you free."

[1] Father Tom Maguire, the well-known Catholc controversialist.

Her father gave consent to let me out on bail,
And I was to stand for trial for his daughter Mary Neal.

Her father kept her close confined, for fear I should her see,
And on my trial day, was my prosecutor to be;
Like a moving beauty bright, to appear she did not fail,
She freed me from all danger, she 's my charming Mary Neal.

With wrath and indignation, her father loud did call,
And when my trial was over, I approached the garden wall,
My well-known voice soon reached her ears, which echoed hill
    and dale,
Saying, " You 're welcome here, my Johnny dear," says charm-
    ing Mary Neal.

We both sat on a sunny bank, and there we talked awhile.
He says, " My dear, if you will comply, I 'll free you from
    exile :
The Shamrock is ready from Derry to set sail;
So come with me, off to Quebec, my charming Mary Neal."

She gave consent, and back she went, and stole the best of
    clothes,
And to no one in the house her secret she made known;
Five hundred pounds of ready gold from her father she did
    steal,
And that was twice I did elope with charming Mary Neal.

Our coach it was got ready to Derry for to go,
And there we bribed the coachman for to let no one know;
He said he would keep secret, and never would reveal.
So off to Derry there I went with charming Mary Neal.

It was to Captain Nelson our passage money paid,
And in the town of Derry it was under cover laid.
We joined our hands in wedlock bands before we did set sail,
And her father's wrath I value not—I love my Mary Neal.

It was over the proud and swelling seas our ship did gently
    glide,
And on our passage to Quebec, six weeks a matchless tide;
Until we came to Whitehead Beach we had no cause to wail,
On Crossford Bay I thought that day I lost my Mary Neal.

On the ninth of June, in the afternoon, a heavy fog came on;
The captain cries, " Look out, my boys! I fear we are all gone."

Our vessel on a sandy bank was driven by a gale,
And forty more washed overboard, along with Mary Neal.

With the help of boats and ship's crew, five hundred they were
saved,
And forty more of them also have met a watery grave.
Her yellow locks I soon espied came floating on the gale,
I jumped into the raging deep and saved my Mary Neal.

Her father wrote me a letter as you may understand,
That if I would go back again he would give me all his land.
I wrote him back an answer, and that without fail,
" That I 'm the heir of your whole estate by your daughter
Mary Neal."

COLLEEN RUE.[1]

As I roved out one summer's morning, speculating most
curiously,
To my surprise, I soon espied a charming fair one approach-
ing me;
I stood awhile in deep meditation, contemplating what should
I do,
But recruiting all my sensations, I thus accosted the *Colleen
Rue:*—

" Are you Aurora, or the beauteous Flora, Euterpasia, or
Venus bright?
Or Helen fair, beyond compare, that Paris stole from her
Grecian's sight?
Thou fairest creature, you have enslaved me, I am intoxicated
by Cupid's clue,
Whose golden notes and infatuation deranged my ideas for
you, *Colleen Rue.*"

" Kind sir, be easy, and do not tease me, with your false praise
so jestingly,
Your dissimulations and invitations, your fantastic praises,
seducing me.
I am not Aurora, or the beauteous Flora, but a rural maiden
to all men's view,
That 's here condoling my situation, and my appellation is the
Colleen Rue."

[1] *Cáilín Ruadh*, red (haired) girl.

"Was I Hector, that noble victor, who died a victim of Grecian
    skill,
Or was I Paris, whose deeds were various, as an arbitrator on
    Ida's hill,
I would roam through Asia, likewise Arabia, through Penn-
    sylvania seeking you,
The burning regions, like famed Vesuvius, for one embrace of
    the *Colleen Rue*."

"Sir, I am surprised and dissatisfied at your tantalizing inso-
    lence,
I am not so stupid, or enslaved by Cupid, as to be dupèd by
    your eloquence,
Therefore desist from your solicitations, I am engaged, I de-
    clare it's true,
To a lad I love beyond all earthly treasures, and he'll soon
    embrace his *Colleen Rue*."

THE CROPPY BOY.

It was very early in the spring,
The birds did whistle and sweetly sing,
Changing their notes from tree to tree,
And the song they sang was old Ireland free.

It was early in the night,
The yeoman cavalry gave me a fright;
The yeoman cavalry was my downfall,
And taken was I by Lord Cornwall.

'T was in the guard-house where I was laid,
And in a parlor where I was tried;
My sentence passed and my courage low
When to Dungannon I was forced to go.

As I was passing by my father's door,
My brother William stood at the door;
My aged father stood at the door,
And my tender mother her hair she tore.

As I was walking up Wexford Street
My own first cousin I chanced to meet;
My own first cousin did me betray,
And for one bare guinea swore my life away.

My sister Mary heard the express,
She ran upstairs in her mourning-dress—
Five hundred guineas I will lay down,
To see my brother through Wexford Town.

As I was walking up Wexford Hill,
Who could blame me to cry my fill?
I looked behind and I looked before,
But my tender mother I shall ne'er see more.

As I was mounted on the platform high,
My aged father was standing by;
My aged father did me deny,
And the name he gave me was the Croppy Boy.

It was in Dungannon this young man died,
And in Dungannon his body lies;
All you good Christians that do pass by
Just drop a tear for the Croppy Boy.

THE CRUISKEEN LAWN.[1]

Let the farmer praise his grounds,
Let the huntsman praise his hounds,
  The shepherd his dew-scented lawn;
But I, more blest than they,
Spend each happy night and day
  With my charming little crúiscín lán, lán, lán,[2]
  My charming little crúiscín lán.

Grádh mo chroidhe mo crúiscín,—
Sláinte geal mo mhúirnín.
  Is grádh mo chroidhe a cúilin bán.

[1] The chorus is pronounced thus :

> Grá-ma-chree ma crooskeen,
> Shlántya gal ma-voorneen
> S grá-ma-chree a cooleen bán.

and means :

> Love of my heart, my little jug!
> Bright health to my darling!
> The love of my heart is her fair hair, etc.

[2] *Lan.* full.

Grádh mo chroidhe mo crúiscín,—
Sláinte geal mo mhúirín,
   Is grádh mo chroidhe a cúilin, bán, bán,
   Is grádh mo chroidhe a cúilin bán.

Immortal and divine,
Great Bacchus, god of wine,
   Create me by adoption your son;
In hope that you 'll comply,
My glass shall ne'er run dry,
   Nor my smiling little crúiscín lán, lán,
   My smiling little crúiscín lán.

And when grim Death appears,
In a few but pleasant years,
   To tell me that my glass has run;
I 'll say, Begone, you knave,
For bold Bacchus gave me lave
   To take another crúiscín lán, lán, lán, lán,
   Another little crúiscín lán.

Then fill your glasses high,
Let 's not part with lips adry,
   Though the lark now proclaims it is dawn;
And since we can 't remain,
May we shortly meet again,
   To fill another crúiscín lán, lán, lán,
   To fill another crúiscín, lán.

THE DEAR AND DARLING BOY.[1]

When first unto this town I came,
   With you I fell in love,
And if I could but gain you
   I 'd vow I 'll never rove.
There 's not a girl in all this town
   I love as well as thee.
I 'll rowl you in my arms,
   My *cushla gal ma chree.*

My love she won't come nigh me,
   Nor hear the moan I make;

[1] This is from a bunch of modern ballads, evidently, from the use of the term "French Flanders," of considerable antiquity.

Neither would she pity me
   Tho' my poor heart should break.
If I was born of noble blood,
   And she of low degree,
She would hear my lamentation,
   And surely pity me.

The ship is on the ocean,
   Now ready for to sail.
If the wind blew from the east,
   With a sweet and pleasant gale;
If the wind blew from my love
   With a sweet and pleasant sound,
It's for your sake, my darling girl,
   I'd range the nations round.

Nine months we are on the ocean,
   No harbor can we spy.
We sailed from the French Flanders
   To harbors that were nigh.
We sailed from the French Flanders
   To harbors that were nigh.

O, fare you well, my darling girl,
   Since you and I must part!
It's the bright beams of your beauty
   That stole away my heart.
But since it is my lot, my love,
   To say that I must go,
Bright angels be your safeguard
   Till my return home.

————

DRIMMIN DUBH DHEELISH.[1]

Oh, there was a poor man,
   And he had but one cow,
And when he had lost her
   He could not tell how,
But so white was her face,
   And so sleek was her tail,
That I thought my poor *drimmin dubh*
   Never would fail.

[1] *Drimmin . . . dheelish*, loyal black white-back.

Agus oro, Drimmin dubh, Oro, ah.
Oro, drimmin dubh, Miel agra.[1]

Returning from mass,
  On a morning in May,
I met my poor *drimmin dubh*
  Drowning by the way.
I roared and I bawled,
  And my neighbors did call
To save my poor *drimmin dubh,*
  She being my all.

Ah, neighbors! was this not
  A sorrowful day,
When I gazed on the water
  Where my *drimmin dubh* lay?
With a drone and a drizzen,
  She bade me adieu,
And the answer I made
  Was a loud pillelu.

Poor *drimmin dubh* sank,
  And I saw her no more,
Till I came to an island
  Was close by the shore;
And down on that island
  I saw her again,
Like a bunch of ripe blackberries
  Rolled in the rain.

Arrah, plague take you, *drimmin dubh!*
  What made you die,
Or why did you leave me,
  For what and for why?
I would rather lose Paudeen,
  My *bouchelleen baun,*[2]
Than part with my *drimmin dubh,*
  Now that you 're gone.

When *drimmin dubh* lived,
  And before she was dead,
She gave me fresh butter
  To eat to my bread,

[1] And choice black white-back.   O choice Ah!
O choice black white-back.   Honey O love!
[2] *Bouchelleen baun*, my little fair-haired boy.

And likewise new milk
  That I soaked with my scone,
But now it's black water
  Since *drimmin dubh's* gone.

GARRYOWEN.

Let Bacchus's sons be not dismayed,
 But join with me each jovial blade;
Come booze and sing, and lend your aid
  To help me with the chorus—
    Instead of Spa we'll drink brown ale,
    And pay the reckoning on the nail,
    No man for debt shall go to jail
     From Garryowen in glory!

We are the boys that take delight in
Smashing the Limerick lamps when lighting,
Through the streets like sporters fighting,
  And tearing all before us.
          Instead, etc.

We'll break windows, we'll break doors,
The watch knock down by threes and fours;
Then let the doctors work their cures,
  And tinker up our bruises.
          Instead, etc.

We'll beat the bailiffs, out of fun,
We'll make the mayor and sheriffs run;
We are the boys no man dares dun,
  If he regards a whole skin.
          Instead, etc.

Our hearts, so stout, have got us fame
For soon 't is known from whence we came;
Where'er we go they dread the name
  Of Garryowen in glory.
          Instead, etc.

Johnny Connell's tall and straight,
And in his limbs he is complete;
He'll pitch a bar of any weight,
  From Garryowen to Thomond Gate.
          Instead. etc.

Garryowen is gone to wrack
Since Johnny Connell went to Cork,
Though Darby O'Brien leapt over the dock
In spite of all the soldiers.
                    Instead, etc.

HANNAH HEALY, THE PRIDE OF HOWTH

You matchless nine, to my aid incline,
    Assist my genius while I declare
My lovesick pain for a beauteous dame,
    Whose killing charms did me ensnare;
Sly little Cupid has knocked me stupid;
    In grief I mourn upon my oath;
My frame's declining, I'm so repining
    For Hannah Healy, the pride of Howth.

She's tall and slender, both young and tender;
    She's modest, mild, and she's all sublime;
For education in Erin's nation
    There's none to equal this nymph divine;
I wish to gain her, but can't obtain her,
    I'd fondly court her, but yet I'm loath,
Lest I should tease her or once displease her,
    Sweet Hannah Healy, the pride of Howth.

At seventeen this maid serene
    My heart attracted, I must allow;
I thought her surely a goddess purely,
    Or some bright angel, in truth I vow;
Since that I languish, my mind's in anguish,
    A deep decline it has curbed my growth;
None can relieve me, then you can believe me,
    But Hannah Healy, the pride of Howth.

In all Olympus I'm sure no nymph is,
    To equal her that I do admire;
Her lovely features surpasses nature;
    Alas, they set my poor heart on fire;
She exceeds Flora, or bright Aurora,
    Or beauteous Venus from the briny froth;—
I am captivated—I do repeat it—
    By Hannah Healy, the pride of Howth.

Each lovely morning young men keep swarming
  To view this charmer taking the air;
She's so enchanting, they all are panting
  To gain her favor, I do declare;
But still they're fearful, and no way cheerful,
  The greatest hero you'll find him loath,
Nor dare entreat her or supplicate her,
  So bright an angel is the pride of Howth.

I'll drop my writing and my inditing,
  I see it's useless for me to fret;
A pound of trouble, or sorrow double,
  Will ne'er atone for an ounce of debt;
I'll resign courting and all like sporting,
  Cupid and Hymen, I'll shun them both,
And raise my mind from all female kind—
  So adieu, sweet Hannah, the pride of Howth!

———

THE IRISH GRANDMOTHER.[1]

Paddy, agra, run down to the bog, for my limbs are beginning
  to tire,
And see if there's ever a sod at all that's dry enough for a fire:
God be praised! It's terrible times, and granny is weak and
  old,
And the praties black as the winter's face, and the night so
  dark and cold!
It's many a day since I seen the like, but I did one, Pat,
  asthore,
And I prayed to God on my bended knees I might never see
  it more.
'T was the year before the Risin' of Smith O'Brien, you know,
Thirty-two years ago, Paddy,—thirty-two years ago.
Your grandfather—God rest his soul!—went out with the
  boys to fight;
For the bailiffs came with the crowbars, and the sickness came
  with the blight,
An' he said it was better to die like a man, though he held
  but a rusty pike,
Than starve on the roadside, beggin' for food, an' be thrown
  like a dog in the dike.

[1] This ballad made its appearance during the agitation and distress of
the winter of 1879. It was first published in the Dublin *Nation* over the
signature *In Fide Fortis.*

Ochone, ochone! it's a sorrowful tale, but listen afore you go,
For Tim he never came back to me, but I'll see him soon, I know.
Tim Ryan he held a decent farm in the glen o' Cahirmore,
And he tilled the lands the Ryans owned two hundred years before;
An' it's many a time, by the blazing fire, I heard from the priest, Father John
(He was my husband's cousin, *agra,* and he lived to be ninety-one),
That the Ryans were chiefs of the country round till Cromwell, the villain, came,
And battered the walls of the castle and set all the houses aflame;
He came an' he stabled his horses in the abbey of St. Columkille,
An' the mark of his murderin' cannon you may see on the old wall still.
An' he planted a common trooper where the Ryans were chieftains of yore,
An' that was the first o' the breed of him that's now Lord Cahirmore.

Old Father John,—he was ninety-one—it was he that could tell you the story,
An' every name of his kith and kin,—may their souls now rest in glory!
His father was shot in '98 as he stood in the chapel door;
His grandfather was the strongest man in the parish of Cahirmore;
An' thin there was Donough, Donal More, and Turlough on the roll,
An' Kian, boy, that lost the lands because he'd save his soul.

Ochone, machree, but the night is cold, and the hunger in your face.
Hard times are comin', *avic!* God help us with his grace!
Three years before the famine came the agent raised the rent,
But then there was many a helpin' hand, and we struggled on content.
Ochone, ochone! we're lonely now,—now that our need is sore,
For there's none but good Father Mahony that ever comes inside our door.
God bless him for the food he brings an' the blankets that keep us warm!
God bless him for his holy words that shelter us from harm!

This is the month an' the day, Paddy, that my own colleen
went,
She died on the roadside, Paddy, when we were drove out for
the rent;
An' it's well that I remember how she turned to me an'
cried,
" There's never a pain that mayn't be a gain," and crossed
herself and died.
For the Soupers were there with shelter and food if we'd only
tell the lie,
But they fled like the wicked things they were when they saw
poor Kathleen die.
She's prayin' for all of us now, Paddy,—her blessing I know
she's giving!
An' they that have little here below have much, *asthore*, in
heaven!

THE IRISHMAN'S FAREWELL TO HIS COUNTRY.[1]

Oh! farewell, Ireland, I am going across the stormy main,
Where cruel strife will end my life, to see you never again.
'T will break my heart from you to part, *acushla store ma-
chree!*
But I must go full of grief and woe to the shores of America.

On Irish soil my fathers dwelt since the days of Brian Boru,
They paid their rent and lived content, convenient to Carrie-
more,
But the landlord sent on the move my poor father and me:
We must leave our home far away to roam in the fields of
America.

No more at the churchyard, *store machree*, at my mother's
grave I'll kneel.
The tyrants know but little of the woe the poor man has to
feel.
When I look on the spot of ground that is so dear to me,
I could curse the laws that have given me cause to depart to
America.

[1] This ballad made its appearance during the time of the Fenian excite-
ment in 1865, when the peasants expected an expedition from the Irish in
the United States.

O, where are the neighbors, kind and true, that were once the country's pride?

No more will they be seen on the face of the green, nor dance on the green hillside.

It is the stranger's cow that is grazing now, where the people we used to see.

With notice they were served, to be turned out or starved, or banished to America.

O, Erin, *machree,* must our children be exiled all over the earth?

Will they evermore think of you, *astore,* as the land that gave them birth?

Must the Irish yield to the beasts of the field? O, no, *acushla store machree!*

They are coming back in ships with vengeance on their lips from the shores of America.

IRISH MOLLY O.[1]

Oh! who is that poor foreigner that lately came to town,
And like a ghost that cannot rest still wanders up and down?
A poor, unhappy Scottish youth;—if more you wish to know,
His heart is breaking all for love of Irish Molly O!
    She's modest, mild, and beautiful, the fairest I have known—
    The primrose of Ireland—all blooming here alone—
    The primrose of Ireland, for wheresoe'er I go,
    The only one entices me is Irish Molly O!

When Molly's father heard of it, a solemn oath he swore,
That if she'd wed a foreigner he'd never see her more.
He sent for young MacDonald and he plainly told him so—
"I'll never give to such as you my Irish Molly O!"
                She's modest, etc.

MacDonald heard the heavy news—and grievously did say—
"Farewell, my lovely Molly, since I'm banished far away,
A poor forlorn pilgrim I must wander to and fro,
And all for the sake of my Irish Molly O!"
                She's modest, etc.

[1] This ballad has been largely kept alive by virtue of the beautiful and pathetic air to which it is sung.

" There is a rose in Ireland, I thought it would be mine:
But now that she is lost to me, I must for ever pine,
Till death shall come to comfort me, for to the grave I 'll go,
And all for the sake of my Irish Molly O ! "
She 's modest, etc.

" And now that I am dying, this one request I crave,
To place a marble tombstone above my humble grave!
And on the stone these simple words I 'd have engraven so—
' MacDonald lost his life for love of Irish Molly O ! ' "
She 's modest, etc.

JENNY FROM BALLINASLOE.

You lads that are funny, and call maids your honey,
   Give ear for a moment; I 'll not keep you long.
I 'm wounded by Cupid; he has made me stupid;
   To tell you the truth now, my brain 's nearly wrong.
A neat little posy, who does live quite cosy,
   Has kept me unable to go to and fro;
Each day I 'm declining, in love I 'm repining,
   For nice little Jenny from Ballinasloe.

It was in September, I 'll ever remember,
   I went out to walk by a clear river side
For sweet recreation, but, to my vexation,
   This wonder of Nature I quickly espied;
I stood for to view her an hour, I 'm sure:
   The earth could not show such a damsel, I know,
As that little girl, the pride of the world,
   Called nice little Jenny from Ballinasloe.

I said to her: " Darling! this is a nice morning;
   The birds sing enchantingly, which charms the groves;
Their notes do delight me, and you do invite me,
   Along this clear water some time for to rove.
Your beauty has won me, and surely undone me;
   If you won't agree for to cure my sad woe,
So great is my sorrow, I 'll ne'er see to-morrow,
   My sweet little Jenny from Ballinasloe."

" Sir, I did not invite you, nor yet dare not slight you;
   You 're at your own option to act as you please:
I am not ambitious, nor e'er was officious;
   I am never inclined to disdain or to tease.

I love conversation, likewise recreation;
   I'm free with a friend, and I'm cold with a foe;
But virtue's my glory, and will be till I'm hoary,"
   Said nice little Jenny from Ballinasloe.

"Most lovely of creatures! your beautiful features
   Have sorely attracted and captured my heart;
If you won't relieve me, in truth you may b'lieve me,
   Bewildered in sorrow till death I must smart;
I'm at your election, so grant me protection,
   And feel for a creature that's tortured in woe.
One smile it will heal me, one frown it will kill me;
   Sweet, nice little Jenny from Ballinasloe!"

"Sir, yonder's my lover; if he should discover
   Or ever take notice you spoke unto me,
He'd close your existence in spite of resistance;
   Be pleased to withdraw, then, lest he might you see.
You see, he's approaching; then don't be encroaching
   He has his large dog and his gun there also.
Although you're a stranger, I wish you from danger,"
   Said nice little Jenny from Ballinasloe.

I bowed then genteelly, and thanked her quite freely;
   I bid her adieu, and took to the road;
So great was my trouble my pace I did double;
   My heart was oppressed and sank down with the load
For ever I'll mourn for beauteous Jane Curran,
   And ramble about in affection and woe,
And think on the hour I saw that sweet flower,
   My dear little Jenny from Ballinasloe!

JOHNNY, I HARDLY KNEW YE.

While going the road to sweet Athy,
     Hurroo! hurroo!
While going the road to sweet Athy,
     Hurroo! hurroo!
While going the road to sweet Athy,
A stick in my hand and a drop in my eye,
A doleful damsel I heard cry:
   "Och Johnny, I hardly knew ye!
      With drums and guns, and guns and drums
      The enemy nearly slew ye;

My darling dear, you look so queer,
Och, Johnny, I hardly knew ye!

" Where are your eyes that looked so mild?
Hurroo! hurroo!
Where are your eyes that looked so mild?
Hurroo! hurroo!
Where are your eyes that looked so mild,
When my poor heart you first beguiled?
Why did you run from me and the child?
Och, Johnny, I hardly knew ye!
With drums, etc.

" Where are the legs with which you run?
Hurroo! hurroo!
Where are the legs with which you run?
Hurroo! hurroo!
Where are the legs with which you run
When you went to carry a gun?
Indeed, your dancing days are done!
Och, Johnny, I hardly knew ye!
With drums, etc.

" It grieved my heart to see you sail,
Hurroo! hurroo!
It grieved my heart to see you sail,
Hurroo! hurroo!
It grieved my heart to see you sail,
Though from my heart you took leg-bail;
Like a cod you're doubled up head and tail.
Och, Johnny, I hardly knew ye!
With drums, etc.

" You haven't an arm and you haven't a leg,
Hurroo! hurroo!
You haven't an arm and you haven't a leg,
Hurroo! hurroo!
You haven't an arm and you haven't a leg,
You're an eyeless, noseless, chickenless egg;
You'll have to be put wid a bowl to beg:
Och, Johnny, I hardly knew ye!
With drums, etc.

" I'm happy for to see you home,
Hurroo! hurroo!
I'm happy for to see you home,
Hurroo! hurroo!

I 'm happy for to see you home,
All from the island of Sulloon,
So low in flesh, so high in bone;
   Och, Johnny, I hardly knew ye!
                      With drums, etc.

" But sad as it is to see you so,
      Hurroo! hurroo!
But sad as it is to see you so,
      Hurroo! hurroo!
But sad as it is to see you so,
And to think of you now as an object of woe,
Your Peggy 'll still keep ye on as her beau;
   Och, Johnny, I hardly knew ye!
      With drums and guns, and guns and drums
      The enemy nearly slew ye;
      My darling dear, you look so queer,
      Och, Johnny, I hardly knew ye! "

THE LAMENTATION OF HUGH REYNOLDS.[1]

My name is Hugh Reynolds, I come of honest parents;
   Near Cavan I was born, as plainly you may see;
By loving of a maid, one Catherine MacCabe,
   My life has been betrayed; she 's a dear maid to me.[2]

[1] I copied this ballad from a broad-sheet in the collection of Mr. Davis; but could learn nothing of its date, or the circumstances connected with it. It is clearly modern, however, and founded on the story of an abduction, which terminated differently from the majority of these adventures. The popular sympathy in such cases is generally in favor of the gallant, the impression being that an abduction is never attempted without at least a tacit consent on the part of the girl. Whenever she appears as a willing witness for the prosecution it is said she has been tampered with by her friends, and public indignation falls upon the wrong object. The 'Lamentation' was probably written for or by the ballad singers; but it is the best of its bad class.

The student would do well to compare it with the other street ballads in the collection; and with the simple old traditional ballads, such as ' Shule Aroon' and ' Peggy Bawn,' that he may discover if possible, where the charm lies that recommends strains so rude and naked to the most cultivated minds. These ballads have done what the songs of our greatest lyrical poets have *not* done—delighted both the educated and the ignorant. Whoever hopes for an equally large and contrasted audience must catch their simplicity, directness, and force, or whatever else constitutes their peculiar attraction.—*Note by Sir Charles Gavan Duffy, ' Ballad Poetry of Ireland.'*

[2] " *A dear maid to me.*" His love for her cost him dear.

The country were bewailing my doleful situation,
  But still I 'd expectation this maid would set me free;
But, oh! she was ungrateful, her parents proved deceitful,
  And though I loved her faithful, she 's a dear maid to me.

Young men and tender maidens, throughout this Irish nation,
  Who hear my lamentation, I hope you 'll pray for me;
The truth I will unfold, that my precious blood she sold,
  In the grave I must lie cold; she 's a dear maid to me.

For now my glass is run, and the hour it is come,
  And I must die for love and the height of loyalty:
I thought it was no harm to embrace her in my arms,
  Or take her from her parents; but she 's a dear maid to me.

Adieu, my loving father, and you, my tender mother,
  Farewell, my dearest brother, who has suffered sore for me;
With irons I 'm surrounded, in grief I lie confounded,
  By perjury unbounded! she 's a dear maid to me.

Now, I can say no more; to the Law-board [1] I must go,
  There to take the last farewell of my friends and counterie;
May the angels, shining bright, receive my soul this night,
  And convey me into heaven to the blessed Trinity.

LANIGAN'S BALL.[2]

In the town of Athy one Jeremy Lanigan
  Battered away till he hadn't a pound,
His father he died and made him a man again,
  Left him a house and ten acres of ground!
He gave a grand party to friends and relations
  Who wouldn't forget him if he went to the wall;
And if you 'll just listen, I 'll make your eyes glisten
  With the rows and the ructions of Lanigan's ball.

Myself, to be sure, got free invitations
  For all the nice boys and girls I 'd ask,
And in less than a minute the friends and relations
  Were dancing as merry as bees round a cask.

[1] *Law-board*, gallows.
[2] ' *Lanigan's Ball*.'—A version made up from several, and as near absolute correctness as seems possible.

Miss Kitty O'Hara, the nice little milliner,
  Tipped me the wink for to give her a call,
And soon I arrived with Timothy Glenniher
  Just in time for Lanigan's ball.

There was lashins of punch and wine for the ladies,
  Potatoes and cakes and bacon and tay,
The Nolans, the Dolans, and all the O'Gradys
  Were courting the girls and dancing away.
Songs they sung as plenty as water,
  From 'The Harp that once through Tara's ould Hall,'
To 'Sweet Nelly Gray' and 'The Ratcatcher's Daughter,'
  All singing together at Lanigan's ball.

They were starting all sorts of nonsensical dances,
  Turning around in a nate whirligig;
But Julia and I soon scatthered their fancies,
  And tipped them the twist of a rale Irish jig.
Och mavrone! 't was then she got glad o' me:
  We danced till we thought the old ceilin' would fall,
(For I spent a whole fortnight in Doolan's Academy
  Learning a step for Lanigan's ball).

The boys were all merry, the girls were all hearty,
  Dancin' around in couples and groups,
When an accident happened—young Terence McCarthy
  He dhruv his right foot through Miss Halloran's hoops.
The creature she fainted, and cried " *Millia murther!* "
  She called for her friends and gathered them all;
Ned Carmody swore he 'd not stir a step further,
  But have satisfaction at Lanigan's ball.

In the midst of the row Miss Kerrigan fainted—
  Her cheeks all the while were as red as the rose—
And some of the ladies declared she was painted,
  She took a small drop too much, I suppose.
Her lover, Ned Morgan, so powerful and able,
  When he saw his dear colleen stretched out by the wall
He tore the left leg from under the table,
  And smashed all the china at Lanigan's ball.

Oh, boys, but then was the ructions—
  Myself got a lick from big Phelim McHugh,
But I soon replied to his kind introductions,
  And kicked up a terrible hullabaloo.

Old Casey the piper was near being strangled,
   They squeezed up his pipes, his bellows, and all;
The girls in their ribbons they all got entangled,
   And that put an end to Lanigan's ball.

A LAY OF THE FAMINE.

Hush! hear you how the night wind keens around the craggy
   reek?
Its voice peals high above the waves that thunder in the
   creek.

"Aroon! aroon! arouse thee, and hie thee o'er the moor!
Ten miles away there's bread, they say; to feed the starving
   poor.

"God save thee, Eileen *bawn astor,* and guide thy naked
   feet,
And keep the fainting life in us till thou come back with meat.

"God send the moon to show thee light upon the way so drear,
And mind thou well the rocky dell, and heed the rushy mere."

She kissed her father's palsied hand, her mother's pallid cheek,
And whirled out on the driving storm beyond the craggy reek.

All night she tracks, with bleeding feet, the rugged mountain
   way,
And townsfolks meet her in the street at flushing of the day.

But God is kinder on the moor than man is in the town,
And Eileen quails before the stranger's harsh rebuke and
   frown.

Night's gloom enwraps the hills once more and hides a slender
   form
That shudders o'er the moor again before the driving storm.

No bread is in her wallet stored, but on the lonesome heath
She lifts her empty hands to God, and prays for speedy death.

Yet struggles onward, faint and blind, and numb to hope or
   fear,
Unmindful of the rocky dell or of the rushy mere.

But, ululu! what sight is this?—what forms come by the reek?
As white and thin as evening mist upon the mountain's peak.

Mist-like they glide across the heath—a weird and ghostly
    band;
The foremost crosses Eileen's path, and grasps her by the hand.

"Dear daughter, thou has suffered sore, but we are well
    and free;
For God has ta'en our life from us, nor wills it long to thee.

"So hie thee to our cabin lone, and dig a grave so deep,
And underneath the golden gorse our corpses lay to sleep—

"Else they will come and smash the walls upon our molder-
    ing bones,
And screaming mountain birds will tear our flesh from out the
    stones.

"And, daughter, haste to do thy work, so thou mayest quickly
    come,
And take with us our grateful rest, and share our peaceful
    home."

The sun behind the distant hills far-sinking down to sleep;
A maiden on the lonesome moor, digging a grave so deep;

The moon above the craggy reek, silvering moor and wave,
And the pale corpse of a maiden young stretched on a new-
    made grave.

MACKENNA'S DREAM.

One night of late I chanced to stray,
All in the pleasant month of May,
When all the Green in slumber lay,
    The moon sunk in the deep;
'T was on a bank I sat me down,
And while the wild wind whistled round,
The ocean with a solemn sound
    Lulled me fast asleep.

I dreamt I saw brave Brian Boru,
Who did the Danish force subdue:

His saber bright with wrath he drew;
    These words he said to me:
"The Harp melodiously shall sound,
When Erin's sons shall be unbound,
St. Patrick's Day they'll dance around
    The blooming laurel tree."

I thought brave Sarsfield drew up nigh,
And presently made this reply,
"For Erin's cause I'll live and die,
    As thousands did before;
My sword again on Aughrim's plain
Old Erin's right shall well maintain,
Through millions in the battle slain,
    And thousands in their gore."

I thought St. Ruth stood on the ground,
And said, "I will your monarch crown,
Encompassed by the French around,
    All ready for the field."
He raised a Cross, and thus did say,
"Brave boys, we'll show them gallant play;
Let no man dare to run away;
    We'll die before we yield."

The Brave O'Byrne he was there,
From Ballymanus, I declare,
Brought Wicklow, Carlow, and Kildare
    To march at his command;
Westmeath and Cavan too did join,
The county Louth men crossed the Boyne,
Slane, Trim, and Navan too did join
    With Dublin to a man.

O'Reilly, on the hill of Screene,
He drew his sword both bright and keen,
And swore by all his eyes had seen,
    He would avenge the fall
Of Erin's sons and daughters brave,
Who nobly filled a martyr's grave,
And died before they'd live enslaved,
    And still for vengeance call.

Then Father Murphy he did say,
"Behold, my lord, I'm here to-day,
With eighteen thousand pikemen gay,
    From Wexford hills so brave:

Our country's fate, it does depend
On you, and on your gallant friend;
And Heaven will his cause defend,
    Who 'll die ere be a slave."

I thought each band played ' Patrick's Day,'
To marshal all in grand array;
With cap and feather white and gay,
    They march in warlike glow,
With drums and trumpets loud and shrill,
And cannon upon every hill;
The pikemen did the valley fill,
    To strike the fatal blow.

When, all at once, appeared in sight
An army clad in armor bright;
Both front, and rear, and left, and right,
    Marched Paddies evermore.
The chieftains pitched their camps with skill,
Determined tyrants' blood to spill;
Beneath us ran a mountain rill,
    As rapid as the Nore.

A Frenchman brave rose up and said—
" Let Erin's sons be not afraid;
To glory I 'll the vanguard lead,
    To honor and renown;
Come, draw your swords along with me,
And let each tyrant bigot see
Dear Erin's daughters must be free
    Before the sun goes down."

Along the line they raised a shout,
Crying, " Quick march, right about! "
With bayonets fixed they all marched out
    To face the deadly foe:
The enemy were no-ways shy,
With thundering cannon planted nigh;
Now thousands on the bank did lie,
    And blood in streams did flow.

The enemy made such a square
As drove our cavalry to despair,
Who were nigh routed, rank and rear,
    But yet not forced to yield.

The Wexford boys that ne'er were slack,
Came, with the brave Tips at their back,
With Longford joined, who in a crack
    Soon sent them off the field.

They gave three cheers for Liberty,
As the enemy all broken flee;
I looked around, but could not see
    One foeman on the plain,
Except the men who wounded lay,
Not able for to run away.
When I awoke 't was break of day—
    So ends MacKenna's dream.

THE MAID OF CLOGHROE.[1]

As I roved out, at Faha, one morning,
  Where Adrum's tall groves were in view—
When Sol's lucid beams were adorning,
  And the meadows were spangled with dew—
Reflecting, in deep contemplation,
  On the state of my country kept low,
I perceived a fair juvenile female
  On the side of the hill of Cloghroe.

Her form resembled fair Venus,
  That amorous Cyprian queen;
She's the charming young sapling of Erin,
  As she gracefully trips on the green;
She's tall, and her form it is graceful,
  Her features are killing also;
She's a charming, accomplished young maiden,
  This beautiful dame of Cloghroe.

Fair Juno, Minerva, or Helen,
  Could not vie with this juvenile dame;
Hibernian swains are bewailing,
  And anxious to know her dear name.
She's tender, she's tall, and she's stately,
  Her complexion much whiter than snow;
She outrivals all maidens completely,
  This lovely young maid of Cloghroe.

[1] *Air—' Cailin deas cruithi-na-mbo,*
    ' The Pretty Girl Milking the Cow.'

At Coachfort, at Dripsey, and Blarney
   This lovely young maid is admired;
The bucks, at the Lakes of Killarney,
   With the fame of her beauty are fired.
Her image, I think, is before me,
   And present wherever I go;
Sweet, charming young maid, I adore thee,
   Thou beautiful nymph of Cloghroe.

Now aid me, ye country grammarians!
   Your learned assistance I claim,
To know the bright name of this fair one—
   This charming young damsel of fame.
To mutes and a liquid united,
   Ingeniously placed in a row,
Spell part of the name of this phœnix,
   This beautiful maid of Cloghroe.

A diphthong and three semivowels
   Will give us this cynosure's name—
This charming Hibernian beauty,
   This lovely, this virtuous young dame.
Had Jupiter heard of this fair one,
   He'd descend from Olympus, I know,
To solicit this juvenile phœnix—
   This beautiful maid of Cloghroe.

MOLLY MULDOON.[1]

Molly Muldoon was an Irish girl,
   And as fine a one
   As you 'd look upon
In the cot of a peasant or hall of an earl.
Her teeth were white, though not of pearl,
And dark was her hair, though it did not curl;
Yet few who gazed on her teeth and her hair,
But owned that a power o' beauty was there.
   Now many a hearty and rattling *gorsoon,*
   Whose fancy had charmed his heart into tune,
   Would dare to approach fair Molly Muldoon,
     But for *that* in her eye
     Which made most of them shy
And look quite ashamed, though they couldn't tell why—

[1] This poem was written about 1850, and its authorship has always been a mystery. It has been ascribed to Fitzjames O'Brien.

Her eyes were large, dark blue, and clear.
    And heart and mind seemed in them blended.
If *intellect* sent you one look severe,
    Love instantly leapt in the next to mend it.
Hers was the eye to check the rude,
    And hers the eye to stir emotion,
To keep the sense and soul subdued,
    And calm desire into devotion.

There was Jemmy O'Hare,
    As fine a boy as you'd see in a fair,
And wherever Molly was he was there.
His face was round and his build was square,
    And he sported as rare
    And tight a pair
Of legs to be sure, as are found anywhere.
    And Jemmy would wear
    His *caubeen* and hair
With such a peculiar and rollicking air,
    That I'd venture to swear
    Not a girl in Kildare,
Nor Victoria's self, if she chanced to be there,
Could resist his wild way—called " Devil may care."
Not a boy in the parish could match him for fun,
Nor wrestle, nor leap, nor hurl, nor run
With Jemmy—no *gorsoon* could equal him—none.
At wake or at wedding, at feast or at fight,
At throwing the sledge with such dext'rous sleight,—
He was the envy of men, and the women's delight.

Now Molly Muldoon liked Jemmy O'Hare,
    And in troth Jemmy loved in his heart Miss Muldoon.
I believe in my conscience a purtier pair
    Never danced in a tent at a patthern in June,—
        To a bagpipe or fiddle
    On the rough cabin-door
        That is placed in the middle—
    Ye may talk as ye will,
There's a grace in the limbs of the peasantry there
With which people of quality couldn't compare.
    And Molly and Jemmy were counted the two
    That could keep up the longest and go the best through
    All the jigs and the reels
        That have occupied heels
Since the days of the Murtaghs and Brian Boru.

It was on a long bright sunny day
  They sat on a green knoll side by side,
But neither just then had much to say;
  Their hearts were so full that they only tried
  To do anything foolish, just to hide
  What both of them felt, but what Molly denied.
They plucked the speckled daisies that grew
Close by their arms,—then tore them too;
And the bright little leaves that they broke from the stalk
They threw at each other for want of talk;
While the heart-lit look and the sunny smile,
Reflected pure souls without art or guile;
  And every time Molly sighed or smiled,
  Jem felt himself grow as soft as a child;
And he fancied the sky never looked so bright,
The grass so green, the daisies so white;
Everything looked so gay in his sight
That gladly he'd linger to watch them till night—
  And Molly herself thought each little bird,
  Whose warbling notes her calm soul stirred,—
  Sang only his lay but by her to be heard.

An Irish courtship's short and sweet,
It's sometimes foolish and indiscreet;
But who is wise when his young heart's heat
Whips the pulse to a galloping beat—
Ties up the judgment neck and feet,
  And makes him the slave of a blind conceit?
Sneer not therefore at the loves of the poor,
Though their manners be rude, their affections are pure;
They look not by art, and they love not by rule,
For their souls are not tempered in fashion's cold school.
Oh! give me the love that endures no control
But the delicate instinct that springs from the soul,
As the mountain stream gushes in freshness and force,
Yet obedient, wherever it flows, to its source.
Yes, give me the love that but Nature has taught,
By rank unallured and by riches unbought;
Whose very simplicity keeps it secure—
The love that illuminates the hearts of the poor.

All blushful was Molly, or shy at least,
    As one week before Lent
    Jem procured her consent
To go the next Sunday and speak to the priest.
  Shrove Tuesday was named for the wedding to be,

And it dawned as bright as they 'd wish to see.
And Jemmy was up at the day's first peep,
For the livelong night no wink could he sleep.
A bran-new coat, with a bright big button,
He took from a chest and carefully put on—
And brogues as well lamp-blacked as ever went foot on,
Were greased with the fat of *a quare sort of mutton!*
Then a tidier *gorsoon* couldn't be seen
Treading the Emerald Isle so green—
Light was his step, and bright was his eye,
As he walked through the *slobbery* streets of Athy.
And each girl he passed bid " God bless him " and sighed,
While she wished in her heart that herself was the bride.

Hush! here 's the Priest—let not the least
Whisper be heard till the Father has ceased.
 " Come, bridegroom and bride,
 That the knot may be tied
 Which no power on earth can hereafter divide."
Up rose the bride and the bridegroom too,
And a passage was made for them both to walk through;
 And his Riv'rence stood with a sanctified face,
 Which spread its infection around the place.
 The bridegroom blushed and whispered the bride,
 Who felt so confused that she almost cried,
 But at last bore up and walked forward, where
 The Father was standing with solemn air;
 The bridegroom was following after with pride,
 When his piercing eye something awful espied!
  He stopped and sighed,
  Looked round and tried
 To tell what he saw, but his tongue denied;
  With a spring and a roar
  He jumped to the door,
AND THE BRIDE LAID HER EYES ON THE BRIDEGROOM NO MORE!

  Some years sped on,
  Yet heard no one
 Of Jemmy O'Hare, or where he had gone.
But since the night of that widowed feast,
The strength of poor Molly had ever decreased;
Till, at length, from earth's sorrow her soul released,
Fled up to be ranked with the saints at least.
And the morning poor Molly to live had ceased,
Just five years after the widowed feast,
An American letter was brought to the priest,

41

Telling of Jemmy O'Hare deceased!
   Who, ere his death,
   With his latest breath,
To a spiritual father unburdened his breast,
And the cause of his sudden departure confest.—
  "Oh, Father," says he, "I 've not long to live,
So I 'll freely confess, and hope you 'll forgive—
That same Molly Muldoon, sure I loved her indeed;
Ay, as well as the Creed
That was never forsaken by one of my breed;
But I couldn't have married her, after I saw—"
  "Saw what?" cried the Father, desirous to hear—
  And the chair that he sat in unconsciously rocking-
"Not in her *karácter,* yer Riv'rince, a flaw"—
The sick man here dropped a significant tear,
And died as he whispered in the clergyman's ear—
But I saw, God forgive her, A HOLE IN HER STOCKING!

THE MORAL.

   Lady readers, love may be
   Fixed in hearts immovably,
   May be strong and may be pure;
   Faith may lean on faith secure,
   Knowing adverse fate's endeavor
   Makes that faith more firm than ever;
   But the purest love and strongest,
   Love that has endured the longest,
   Braving cross, and blight, and trial,
   Fortune's bar or pride's denial,
   Would—no matter what its trust—
   Be uprooted by disgust:—
   Yes, the love that might for years
   Spring in suffering, grow in tears,
   Parents' frigid counsel mocking,
   Might be—where 's the use of talking?—
   Upset by a BROKEN STOCKING!

THE NATIVE IRISHMAN.

BY A CONVERTED SAXON.

Before I came across the sea
  To this delightful place,
I thought the native Irish were
  A funny sort of race;

I thought they bore shillelagh-sprigs,
  And that they always said:
" Och hone, acushla, tare-an-ouns,"
    " Begorra," and " bedad!"

I thought they sported crownless hats
  With dhudeens in the rim;
I thought they wore long trailing coats
  And knickerbockers trim;
I thought they went about the place
  As tight as they could get;
And that they always had a fight
  With every one they met.

I thought their noses all turned up
  Just like a crooked pin;
I thought their mouths six inches wide
  And always on the grin;
I thought their heads were made of stuff
  As hard as any nails;
I half suspected that they were
  Possessed of little tails.

.   .   .   .   .

But when I came unto the land
  Of which I heard so much,
I found that the inhabitants
  Were not entirely such;
I found their features were not all
  Exactly like baboons';
I found that some wore billycocks,
  And some had pantaloons.

I found their teeth were quite as small
  As Europeans' are,
And that their ears, in point of size,
  Were not pecul-iar.
I even saw a face or two
  Which might be handsome called;
And by their very largest feet
  I was not much appalled.

I found them sober, now and then;
  And even in the street,
It seems they do not have a fight
  With every boy they meet.

I even found some honest men
  Among the very poor;
And I have heard some sentences
  Which did not end with " shure."

It seems that praties in their skins
  Are not their only food,
And that they have a house or two
  Which is not built of mud.
In fact, they 're not all brutes or fools,
  And I suspect that when
They rule themselves they 'll be as good,
  Almost, as Englishmen!

NELL FLAHERTY'S DRAKE.[1]

My name it is Nell, quite candid I tell,
  That I live near Coote hill, I will never deny;
I had a fine drake, the truth for to spake,
  That my grandmother left me and she going to die;
He was wholesome and sound, he would weigh twenty pound,
  The universe round I would rove for his sake—
Bad wind to the robber—be he drunk or sober—
  That murdered Nell Flaherty's beautiful drake.

His neck it was green—most rare to be seen,
  He was fit for a queen of the highest degree;
His body was white—and would you delight—
  He was plump, fat and heavy, and brisk as a bee.
The dear little fellow, his legs they were yellow,
  He would fly like a swallow and dive like a hake,
But some wicked savage, to grease his white cabbage,
  Has murdered Nell Flaherty's beautiful drake.

May his pig never grunt, may his cat never hunt,
  May a ghost ever haunt him at dead of the night;
May his hen never lay, may his ass never bray,
  May his goat fly away like an old paper kite.
That the flies and the fleas may the wretch ever tease,
  And the piercing north breeze make him shiver and shake,
May a lump of a stick raise bumps fast and thick
  On the monster that murdered Nell Flaherty's drake.

[1] Many versions of this ballad are to be found in the Irish ballad-slips. They are all corrupt and generally very gross. Note its similarity to O'Kelly's ' Curse of Doneraile.'

May his cradle ne'er rock, may his box have no lock,
  May his wife have no frock for to cover her back;
May his cock never crow, may his bellows ne'er blow,
  And his pipe and his pot may he evermore lack.
May his duck never quack, may his goose turn black,
  And pull down his turf with her long yellow beak;
May the plague grip the scamp, and his villainy stamp
  On the monster that murdered Nell Flaherty's drake.

May his pipe never smoke, may his teapot be broke,
  And to add to the joke, may his kettle ne'er boil;
May he keep to the bed till the hour that he's dead,
  May he always be fed on hogwash and boiled oil.
May he swell with the gout, may his grinders fall out,
  May he roll, howl and shout with the horrid toothache;
May the temples wear horns, and the toes many corns,
  Of the monster that murdered Nell Flaherty's drake.

May his spade never dig, may his sow never pig,
  May each hair in his wig be well thrashed with a flail;
May his door have no latch, may his house have no thatch,
  May his turkey not hatch, may the rats eat his meal.
May every old fairy, from Cork to Dunleary,
  Dip him snug and airy in river or lake,
Where the eel and the trout may feed on the snout
  Of the monster that murdered Nell Flaherty's drake.

May his dog yelp and howl with the hunger and could,
  May his wife always scold till his brains go astray;
May the curse of each hag that e'er carried a bag
  Alight on the vag, till his hair turns gray.
May monkeys affright him, and mad dogs still bite him,
  And every one slight him, asleep or awake;
May weasels still gnaw him, and jackdaws still claw him—
  The monster that murdered Nell Flaherty's drake.

The only good news that I have to infuse
  Is that old Peter Hughes and blind Peter McCrake,
And big-nosed Bob Manson, and buck-toothed Ned Hanson,
  Each man had a grandson of my lovely drake.
My treasure had dozens of nephews and cousins,
  And one I must get or my heart it will break;
To keep my mind easy, or else I'll run crazy—
  This ends the whole song of my beautiful drake.

45

The night before Larry was stretched,
  The boys they all paid him a visit;
A bait in their sacks, too, they fetched;
  They sweated their duds till they riz it:
For Larry was ever the lad,
  When a boy was condemned to the squeezer,
Would fence all the duds that he had
  To help a poor friend to a sneezer,
    And warm his gob 'fore he died.

The boys they came crowding in fast,
  They drew all their stools round about him,
Six glims round his trap-case were placed,
  He couldn't be well waked without 'em.
When one of us asked could he die
  Without having duly repented,
Says Larry, " That 's all in my eye;
  And first by the clargy invented,
    To get a fat bit for themselves."

" I 'm sorry, dear Larry," says I,
  " To see you in this situation;
And, blister my limbs if I lie,
  I 'd as lieve it had been my own station."
" Ochone! it 's all over," says he,
  " For the neckcloth I 'll be forced to put on
And by this time to-morrow you 'll see
  Your poor Larry as dead as a mutton,"
    Because, why, his courage was good.

" And I 'll be cut up like a pie,
  And my nob from my body be parted."
" You 're in the wrong box, then," says I,
  " For blast me if they 're so hard-hearted:
A chalk on the back of your neck
  Is all that Jack Ketch dares to give you;
Then mind not such trifles a feck,
  For why should the likes of them grieve you?
    And now, boys, come tip us the deck."

The cards being called for, they played,
  Till Larry found one of them cheated;

¹ The authorship of this extraordinary piece of poetic ribaldry has been much discussed, but has never been discovered. It is written in Dublin slang of the end of the eighteenth century.

A dart at his napper he made
  (The boy being easily heated):
" Oh, by the hokey, you thief,
  I 'll scuttle your nob with my daddle!
You cheat me because I 'm in grief,
  But soon I 'll demolish your noddle,
    And leave you your claret to drink."

Then the clergy came in with his book,
  He spoke him so smooth and so civil;
Larry tipped him a Kilmainham look,
  And pitched his big wig to the devil;
Then sighing, he threw back his head
  To get a sweet drop of the bottle,
And pitiful sighing, he said:
  " Oh, the hemp will be soon round my throttle
    And choke my poor windpipe to death.

" Though sure it 's the best way to die,
  Oh, the devil a betther a-livin'!
For, sure, when the gallows is high
  Your journey is shorter to Heaven:
But what harasses Larry the most,
  And makes his poor soul melancholy,
Is to think of the time when his ghost
  Will come in a sheet to sweet Molly—
    Oh, sure it will kill her alive!"

So moving these last words he spoke,
  We all vented our tears in a shower;
For my part, I thought my heart broke,
  To see him cut down like a flower,
On his travels we watched him next day;
  Oh, the throttler! I thought I could kill him;
But Larry not one word did say,
  Nor changed till he come to " King William "—
    Then, *musha!* his color grew white.

When he came to the nubbling chit,
  He was tucked up so neat and so pretty,
The rumbler jogged off from his feet,
  And he died with his face to the city;
He kicked, too—but that was all pride,
  For soon you might see 't was all over;
Soon after the noose was untied,
  And at darky we waked him in clover,
    And sent him to take a ground sweat.

In the gold vale of Limerick,
  Beside the Shannon stream,
The maiden lives who holds my heart,
  And haunts me like a dream,
With shiny showers of golden hair
  And gentle as a fawn,
The cheeks that make the red rose pale,
  My darling Colleen Bawn.

Although she seldom speaks to me,
  I think on her with pride;
For five long years I courted her,
  And asked her to be my bride.
But dreary times of cold neglect
  Are all from her I 've drawn,
For I am but a laboring boy,
  And she the Colleen Bawn.

Her hands are whiter than the snow
  Upon the mountain side,
And softer than the creamy foam,
  That floats upon the tide;
Her eyes are brighter than the snow
  That sparkles on the lawn;
The sunshine of my life is she,
  The darling Colleen Bawn.

To leave old Ireland far behind
  Is often in my mind,
And wander for another bride
  And country for to find,
But that I 've seen a low suitor
  Upon her footsteps fawn,
Which keeps me near to guard my dear,
  My darling Colleen Bawn.

Her beauty very far excels
  All other females fine;
She is far brighter than the sun
  That does upon us shine;
Each night she does disturb my rest,
  I cannot sleep till dawn,

¹ This is from a bunch of Dublin street ballads of the nineteenth century, but its date of composition is of course uncertain.

Still wishing her to be my bride,
  My darling Colleen Bawn.

The women of Limerick take the sway
  Throughout old Erin's shore;
They fought upon the city walls,
  They did in days of yore.
They kept away the enemy
  All night until the dawn:
Most worthy of the title is
  My darling Colleen Bawn.

PROTESTANT BOYS.

AN ORANGE SONG.

Tell me, my friends, why are we met here?
  Why thus assembled, ye Protestant Boys?
Do mirth and good liquor, good humor, good cheer,
  Call us to share of festivity's joys?
        O no! 't is the cause
        Of King—Freedom—and Laws,
That calls loyal Protestants now to unite;
        And Orange and Blue,
        Ever faithful and true,
Our King shall support, and Sedition affright.

Great spirit of William! from Heaven look down,
  And breathe in our hearts our forefathers' fire—
Teach us to rival their glorious renown,
  From Papist or Frenchman ne'er to retire.
        Jacobin—Jacobite—
        Against all to unite.
Who dare to assail our Sovereign's throne?
        For Orange and Blue
        Will be faithful and true,
And Protestant loyalty ever be shown.

In that loyalty proud let us ever remain,
  Bound together in Truth and Religion's pure band;
Nor Honor's fair cause with foul Bigotry stain,
  Since in Courage and Justice supported we stand.
        So Heaven shall smile
        On our emerald isle.

And lead us to conquest again and again;
While Papists shall prove
Our brotherly love:—
We hate them as masters—we love them as men.

By the deeds of their fathers to glory inspired,
Our Protestant heroes shall combat the foe;
Hearts with true honor and loyalty fired,
Intrepid, undaunted, to conquest will go.
In Orange and Blue,
Still faithful and true,
The soul-stirring music of glory they 'll sing;
The shades of the Boyne
In the chorus will join,
And the welkin re-echo with " God save the King."

THE RAKES OF MALLOW.

Beauing, belling, dancing, drinking,
Breaking windows, damning, sinking,[1]
Ever raking, never thinking,
     Live the rakes of Mallow.

Spending faster than it comes,
Beating waiters, bailiffs, duns,
Bacchus's true-begotten sons,
     Live the rakes of Mallow.

One time nought but claret drinking,
Then like politicians thinking
To raise the sinking funds when sinking,
     Live the rakes of Mallow.

When at home with dadda dying,
Still for Mallow water crying;
But where there's good claret plying,
     Live the rakes of Mallow.

Living short but merry lives;
Going where the devil drives;
Having sweethearts, but no wives,
     Live the rakes of Mallow.

[1] *Sinking*, cursing extravagantly—*i.e.* damning you to hell and *sinking* you lower.

Racking tenants, stewards teasing,
Swiftly spending, slowly raising,
Wishing to spend all their days in
Raking as at Mallow.

Then to end this raking life
They get sober, take a wife,
Ever after live in strife,
And wish again for Mallow.

THE SHAN VAN VOCHT.[1]

Oh! the French are on the sea,
    Says the Shan Van Vocht;
The French are on the sea,
    Says the Shan Van Vocht;
Oh! the French are in the Bay,
They 'll be here without delay,
And the Orange will decay,
    Says the Shan Van Vocht.

Oh! the French are in the Bay,
They 'll be here by break of day,
And the Orange will decay,
    Says the Shan Van Vocht.

And where will they have their camp?
    Says the Shan Van Vocht;
Where will they have their camp?
    Says the Shan Van Vocht;
On the Curragh of Kildare,
The boys they will be there,
With their pikes in good repair,
    Says the Shan Van Vocht.

To the Curragh of Kildare,
The boys they will repair,
And Lord Edward will be there,
    Says the Shan Van Vocht.

Then what will the yeomen do?
    Says the Shan Van Vocht;

[1] *Shan Van Vocht*, " The Poor Old Woman"—a name for Ireland. This
was written in 1896, when the French fleet arrived in Bantry Bay.

What will the yeomen do?
   Says the Shan Van Vocht;
What should the yeomen do,
But throw off the red and blue,
And swear that they 'll be true
   To the Shan Van Vocht?

What should the yeomen do,
But throw off the red and blue,
And swear that they 'll be true
   To the Shan Van Vocht?

And what color will they wear?
   Says the Shan Van Vocht;
What color will they wear?
   Says the Shan Van Vocht;
What color should be seen
Where our fathers' homes have been,
But their own immortal Green?
   Says the Shan Van Vocht.

What color should be seen
Where our fathers' homes have been,
But their own immortal Green?
   Says the Shan Van Vocht.

And will Ireland then be free?
   Says the Shan Van Vocht;
Will Ireland then be free?
   Says the Shan Van Vocht;
Yes! Ireland shall be free,
From the center to the sea;
Then hurrah for Liberty!
   Says the Shan Van Vocht.

Yes! Ireland shall be free,
From the center to the sea;
Then hurrah for Liberty!
   Says the Shan Van Vocht.

A BRIGADE BALLAD.

I would I were on yonder hill,
'T is there I 'd sit and cry my fill,
And every tear would turn a mill,
Is go d-teidh tu, a mhúrnin, slán!

> *Siubhail, siubhail, siubhail, a rúin!*
> *Siubhail go socair, agus siubhail go ciúin,*
> *Siubhail go d-ti an doras agus eulaigh liom,*
> *Is go d-teidh tu, a mhúrnin, slán!*

I 'll sell my rock, I 'll sell my reel,
I 'll sell my only spinning-wheel,
To buy for my love a sword of steel,
Is go d-teidh tu, a mhúrnin, slán!
                              Siubhail etc.

I 'll dye my petticoats, I 'll dye them red,
And round the world I 'll beg my bread,
Until my parents shall wish me dead,
Is go d-teidh tu, a mhúrnin, slán!
                              Siubhail etc.

I wish, I wish, I wish in vain,
I wish I had my heart again,
And vainly think I 'd not complain,
Is go d-teidh tu, a mhúrnin, slán!
                              Siubhail etc.

But now my love has gone to France,
To try his fortune to advance;
If he e'er come back, 't is but a chance,
Is go d-teidh tu, a mhúrnin, slán!
                              Siubhail etc.

[1] The date of this ballad is not positively known, but it appears to be early in the eighteenth century, when the flower of the Catholic youth of Ireland were drawn away to recruit the ranks of the Brigade. The inexpressible tenderness of the air, and the deep feeling and simplicity of the words, have made the ballad a popular favorite, notwithstanding its meagerness and poverty.—*Note by Sir Charles Gavan Duffy, 'Ballad Poetry of Ireland.'*

[2] In Sparling's 'Irish Minstrelsy' this is versified almost literally, as follows:

> "Come, come, come, O Love!
> Quickly come to me, softly move;
> Come to the door, and away we 'll flee,
> And safe for aye may my darling be!"

THE SORROWFUL LAMENTATION OF CALLAGHAN, GREALLY, AND MULLEN.[1]

"Come, tell me, dearest mother, what makes my father stay,
Or what can be the reason that he's so long away?"
"Oh! hold your tongue, my darling son, your tears do grieve
    me sore;
I fear he has been murdered in the fair of Turloughmore."

Come, all you tender Christians, I hope you will draw near;
It's of this dreadful murder I mean to let you hear,
Concerning those poor people whose loss we do deplore
(The Lord have mercy on their souls) that died at Turlough-
    more.

It is on the First of August, the truth I will declare,
Those people they assembled that day all at the fair;
But little was their notion what evil was in store,
All by the bloody Peelers at the fair of Turloughmore.

Were you to see that dreadful sight 't would grieve your heart,
    I know,
To see the comely women and the men all lying low;
God help their tender parents, they will never see them more,
For cruel was their murder at the fair of Turloughmore.

It's for that base bloodthirsty crew, remark the word I say,
The Lord He will reward them against the judgment day;
The blood they have taken innocent, for it they'll suffer sore,
And the treatment that they gave to us that day at Turlough-
    more.

[1] This is a genuine ballad of the people, written and sung among them.
The reader will see at once how little resemblance it bears to the *pseudo*
Irish songs of the stage, or even to the street ballads manufactured by the
ballad singers. It is very touching, and not without a certain unpremed-
itated grace. The vagueness, which leaves entirely untold the story it
undertook to recount, is a common characteristic of the Anglo-Irish songs
of the people. The circumstance on which it is founded took place in 1843,
at the fair of Darrynacloughery, held at Turloughmore. A faction fight
having occurred at the fair, the arrest of some of the parties led to an
attack on the police; after the attack had abated or ceased, the police
fired on the people, wounded several, and killed the three men whose
names stand at the head of the ballad. They were indicted for murder,
and pleaded the order of Mr. Brew, the stipendiary magistrate, which was
admitted as justification. Brew died before the day appointed for his
trial.—*Note by Sir Charles Gavan Duffy, 'Ballad Poetry of Ireland.'*

The morning of their trial as they stood up in the dock,
The words they spoke were feeling, the people round them
  flock;
" I tell you, Judge and Jury, the truth I will declare,
It was Brew that ordered us to fire that evening at the fair."

Now to conclude and finish this sad and doleful fray,
I hope their souls are happy against the judgment day;
It was little time they got, we know, when they fell like new-
  mowed hay,
May the Lord have mercy on their souls against the judgment
  day.

THE STAR OF SLANE.

Ye brilliant muses, who ne'er refuses,
  But still infuses in the poet's mind,
Your kind sweet favors to his endeavors,
  That his ardent labors should appear sublime;
Preserve my study from getting muddy,
  My idea's ready, so inspire my brain;
My quill refine, as I write each line,
  On a nymph divine called the Star of Slane.

In beauteous Spring, when the warblers sing,
  And their carols ring through each fragrant grove;
Bright Sol did shine, which made me incline
  By the river Boyne for to go to rove,
I was ruminating and meditating
  And contemplating as I paced the plain,
When a charming fair, beyond compare,
  Did my heart ensnare near the town of Slane.

Had Paris seen this young maid serene,
  The Grecian queen he would soon disdain,
And straight embrace this virgin chaste,
  And peace would grace the whole Trojan plain.
If Ancient Cæsar could on her gaze, sir,
  He'd stand amazed for to view this dame;
Sweet Cleopatra he would freely part her,
  And his crown he'd barter for the Star of Slane.

There's Alexander, that famed commander,
  Whose triumphant standard it did conquer all,

Who proved a victor over crowns and scepters,
  And great warlike structures did before him fall
Should he behold her, I will uphold, sir,
  From pole to pole he would then proclaim,
For the human race in all that wide space,
  To respect the chaste blooming Star of Slane.

To praise her beauty then is my duty,
  But alas! I 'm footy [1] in this noble part,
And to my sorrow, sly Cupid's arrow
  Full deep did burrow in my tender heart;
In pain and trouble yet I will struggle,
  Though sadly hobbled by my stupid brain,
Yet backed by Nature I can tell each feature
  Of this lovely creature called the Star of Slane.

Her eyes it 's true are an azure blue,
  And her cheeks the hue of the crimson rose;
Her hair behold it does shine like gold,
  And is finely rolled and so nicely grows;
Her skin is white as the snow by night,
  Straight and upright is her supple frame;
The chaste Diana, or fair Susanna,
  Are eclipsed in grandeur by the Star of Slane.

Her name to mention it might cause contention,
  And it 's my intention for to breed no strife;
For me to woo her I am but poor,
  I 'm deadly sure she won't be my wife;
In silent anguish I here must languish
  Till time does banish all my love-sick pain,
And my humble station I must bear with patience,
  Since great exaltation suits the Star of Slane.

TIPPERARY RECRUITING SONG.

'T is now we 'd want to be wary, boys,
The recruiters are out in Tipperary, boys;
If they offer a glass, we 'll wink as they pass—
We 're old birds for chaff in Tipperary, boys.

Then, hurrah for the gallant Tipperary boys,
Although we 're " cross and contrary," boys;

[1] *Footy*, poor, mean, insignificant.

The never a one will handle a gun,
Except for the Green and Tipperary, boys.

Now mind what John Bull did here, my boys,
In the days of our famine and fear, my boys;
He burned and sacked, he plundered and racked,
Old Ireland of Irish to clear, my boys.

Now Bull wants to pillage and rob, my boys,
And put the proceeds in his fob, my boys;
But let each Irish blade just stick to his trade,
And let Bull do his own dirty job, my boys.

So never to 'list be in haste, my boys,
Or a glass of drugged whisky to taste, my boys;
If to India you go, it's to grief and to woe,
And to rot and to die like a beast, my boys.

But now he is beat for men, my boys,
His army is getting so thin, my boys,
With the fever and ague, the sword and the plague,
O, the devil a fear that he'll win, my boys.

Then mind not the nobblin' old schemer, boys,
Though he says that he's richer than Damer, boys;
Though he bully and roar, his power is o'er,
And his black heart will shortly be tamer, boys.

Now, isn't Bull peaceful and civil, boys,
In his mortal distress and his evil, boys?
But we'll cock each *caubeen* when his sergeants are seen,
And we'll tell them to go to the devil, boys.

Then hurrah for the gallant Tipperary boys!
Although " we're cross and contrary," boys;
The never a one will handle a gun,
Except for the Green and Tipperary, boys.

TRUST TO LUCK.[1]

Trust to luck, trust to luck, stare fate in the face,
Sure the heart must be aisy when it's in the right place:

[1] This has for years been a favorite with the street singers and the people, and its refrain has been sung by more than one notable criminal before his execution. as a sort of *Nunc dimittis*.

Let the world wag away, let your friends turn to foes,
Let your pockets run dry and threadbare be your clothes;
Should woman deceive, when you trust to her heart,
Never sigh—'t won't relieve it, but add to the smart.
    Trust to luck, trust to luck, stare fate in the face,
    Sure the heart must be aisy when it's in the right place.

Be a man, be a man, wheresoever you go,
Through the sunshine of wealth, or the teardrop of woe.
Should the wealthy look grand and the proud pass you by
With the back of their hand and the scorn of their eye,
Snap your fingers and smile as you pass on your way,
And remember the while every dog has his day.
    Trust to luck, trust to luck, stare fate in the face,
    Sure the heart must be aisy when it's in the right place.

In love as in war sure it's Irish delight,
He's good-humored with both, the sweet girl and a fight;
He coaxes, he bothers, he blarneys the dear,
To resist him she can't, and he's off when she's near,
And when valor calls him, from his darling he'd fly,
And for liberty fight and for ould Ireland die.
    Trust to luck, trust to luck, stare fate in the face,
    The heart must be aisy, if it's in the right place.

THE WEARIN' O' THE GREEN.

Oh, Paddy dear! an' did ye hear the news that's goin' round?
The shamrock is by law forbid to grow on Irish ground.
No more St. Patrick's Day we'll keep, his color can't be seen,
For there's a cruel law agin the wearin' o' the green!
I met wid Napper Tandy, and he took me by the hand,
And he said, "How's poor Ould Ireland, and how does she
    stand?"
She's the most disthressful country that iver yet was seen,
For they're hangin' men and women there for wearin' o' the
    green.

An' if the color we must wear is England's cruel red,
Let it remind us of the blood that Ireland has shed;
Then pull the shamrock from your hat, and throw it on the
    sod,—
And never fear, 't will take root there, tho' under foot 't is
    trod!

When law can stop the blades of grass from growin' as they
    grow,
And when the leaves in summer-time their color dare not show,
Then I will change the color, too, I wear in my caubeen,
But till that day, plaze God, I 'll stick to wearin' o' the green.

WILLY REILLY.[1]

"Oh! rise up, Willy Reilly, and come along with me,
I mean for to go with you and leave this counterie,
To leave my father's dwelling, his houses and free land;"
And away goes Willy Reilly and his dear *Coolen Ban*.

They go by hills and mountains, and by yon lonesome plain,
Through shady groves and valleys, all dangers to refrain;
But her father followed after with a well-armed band,
And taken was poor Reilly and his dear *Coolen Ban*.

It 's home then she was taken, and in her closet bound;
Poor Reilly all in Sligo jail lay on the stony ground,
Till at the bar of justice, before the Judge he 'd stand,
For nothing but the stealing of his dear *Coolen Ban*.

"Now in the cold, cold iron my hands and feet are bound,
I 'm handcuffed like a murderer, and tied unto the ground.
But all the toil and slavery I 'm willing for to stand,
Still hoping to be succored by my dear *Coolen Ban*."

The jailor's son to Reilly goes, and thus to him did say:
"Oh! get up, Willy Reilly, you must appear this day,
For great Squire Foillard's anger you never can withstand,
I 'm afeered you 'll suffer sorely for your dear *Coolen Ban*.

"This is the news, young Reilly, last night that I did hear:
The lady's oath will hang you or else will set you clear."
"If that be so," says Reilly, "her pleasure I will stand,
Still hoping to be succored by my dear *Coolen Ban*."

---

[1] 'Willy Reilly' was the first ballad I ever heard recited, and it made a
painfully vivid impression on my mind. I have never forgotten the smallest
incident of it. The story on which it is founded happened some sixty
years ago; and as the lover was a young Catholic farmer, and the lady's
family of high Orange principles, it got a party character, which, no doubt,
contributed to its great popularity. There is no family under the rank of
gentry, in the inland counties of Ulster, where it is not familiarly known.
Nurses and sempstresses. the honorary guardians of national songs and
legends, have taken it into special favor, and preserved its popularity.—
Note by Sir Charles Gavan Duffy.

Now Willy 's drest from top to toe all in a suit of green,
His hair hangs o'er his shoulders most glorious to be seen;
He 's tall and straight, and comely as any could be found;
He 's fit for Foillard's daughter, was she heiress to a crown.

The Judge he said: " This lady being in her tender youth,
If Reilly has deluded her she will declare the truth."
Then, like a moving beauty bright before him she did stand,
" You 're welcome there, my heart's delight and dear *Coolen
    Ban.*"

" Oh, gentlemen," Squire Foillard said, " with pity look on me,
This villain came amongst us to disgrace our family,
And by his base contrivances this villainy was planner;
If I don't get satisfactioṇ I 'll quit this Irish land."

The lady with a tear began, and thus replied she:
" The fault is none of Reilly's, the blame lies all on me;
I forced him for to leave this place and come along with me;
I loved him out of measure, which wrought our destiny."

Out bespoke the noble Fox, at the table he stood by:
" Oh gentlemen, consider on this extremity;
To hang a man for love is a murder, you may see:
So spare the life of Reilly, let him leave this counterie."

" Good my lord, he stole from her her diamonds and her rings,
Gold watch and silver buckles, and many precious things,
Which cost me in bright guineas more than five hundred
    pounds,
I 'll have the life of Reilly should I lose ten thousand pounds."

" Good my lord, I gave them him as tokens of true love,
And when we are a-parting I will them all remove;
If you have got them, Reilly, pray send them home to me."
" I will, my loving lady, with many thanks to thee."

" There is a ring among them I allow yourself to wear,
With thirty locket diamonds well set in silver fair,
And as a true-love token wear it on your right hand,
That you 'll think on my poor broken heart when you 're in
    foreign land."

Then out spoke noble Fox: " You may let the prisoner go;
The lady's oath has cleared him, as the Jury all may know.
She has released her own true love, she has renewed his name;
May her honor bright gain high estate, and her offspring rise
    to fame!"